T0082523

Barefoot in Rain

Barefoot in Rain

A Book of Villanelles

Amanullah Khan

 iUniverse®

BAREFOOT IN RAIN
A BOOK OF VILLANELLES

iUniverse books may be ordered through booksellers or by contacting:

iUniverse
1663 Liberty Drive
Bloomington, IN 47403
www.iuniverse.com
844-349-9409

ISBN: 978-1-6632-4630-1 (sc)
ISBN: 978-1-6632-4631-8 (e)

Library of Congress Control Number: 2022918253

Print information available on the last page.

iUniverse rev. date: 09/29/2022

The editorial assistance of Sabrina Khan Perry and
Roxanna Khan Manning is gratefully acknowledged.

To my granddaughters,
Liliana Chugani and Bray Manning

A Note on the Villanelle

The villanelle focuses on a single point, circles around, and brings you back to the same point. Therefore the beauty of a villanelle lies in keeping you focused. The verse form most likely started in the Italian fields at harvest time in the 1600s.

A villanelle has nineteen lines, with five stanzas of three lines each (tercets) and a sixth stanza of four lines (the quatrain).

The rhyme scheme of the tercets is *aba*. The first line of the first tercet is repeated as the last line of the second and fourth. The last line of the first tercet is repeated as the last line of the third and fifth.

The two refrain lines become the third and fourth lines of the last stanza, the quatrain.

Contents

PART 3
CIVILIZATION

PART 4
WARS

PART 5
LOOKING BACK

PART 6
LIFE'S FRAGILITY

PART 1

Writing Villanelles

Writing a Villanelle

I saw a villanelle in a book
Worn out by the passage of time.
I could not free myself from the hook.

Reading an old poem like a schnook,
I finally perceived its rhyme:
I saw a villanelle in a book.

It was like reading a textbook;
It will stay with me for a lifetime.
I could not escape the strong hook.

For the line scheme I needed a book,
Which I could go back to in time:
I saw a villanelle in a book.

I was glad for the time it took,
Till I got it done in good time.
I could not escape the strong hook.

I was happy how long it took;
I finished it in a short time.
I saw a villanelle in a book.
I could not escape the strong hook.

How to Write a Villanelle

To see the grace of the season's belle
(A sheer ecstasy for the mind,
Enough to write a villanelle),

The pen will paint; I cannot tell.
Alluring moment, one of a kind,
To see the grace of the season's belle;

A magic instance, hard to spell:
You are mystified, and you find
Enough to write a villanelle.

Let me give you a hint as well:
The stars will have to be aligned
To see the grace of the season's belle.

To the worries you say farewell;
Sea of bliss, a moment divined
Enough to write a villanelle.

Suddenly she will cast a spell,
And you will shed the daily grind
To see the grace of the season's belle
Enough to write a villanelle.

Weatherman

No one is pleased with the weatherman.
On good days, he can name his price.
They belong to a special clan.

He does his best to spell God's plan.
He might as well just roll the dice—
No one is pleased with the weatherman.

On bad days, he may advise "Suntan!"
Or on a bright day may say "Ice."
They belong to a special clan.

You may as well ask the doorman!
No one answer will be concise.
No one is pleased with the weatherman.

He is a poised and dignified man,
In bad weather giving his advice.
They belong to a special clan.

Gadgets have been improved by man,
So man can give better advice.
No one is pleased with the weatherman—
They belong to a special clan.

Love in the Eyes

She may not say; her eyes will tell.
Eyes will say what is in the heart.
You just sit and finish your villanelle.

What words belie, her eyes will spell.
You will see a pure divine art.
She may not say; her eyes will tell.

When you realize chimes a bell;
You hear pianos play Mozart.
You just sit and finish your villanelle.

You feel that you are in a spell.
If in doubt, look into her eyes.
She may not say; her eyes will tell.

You find yourself in alluring dell,
And you do not wish to depart.
You just sit and finish your villanelle.

You may now end the villanelle—
End it right there, and be smart.
She may not say; her eyes will tell.
You just sit and finish your villanelle.

The Heart is the Abode of God

If you fall in love that is true,
They will try to tear it apart.
The world may come crashing down on you.

God lives in your heart, not just you.
No one has control over your heart,
If you fall in love that is true.

Don't forget, God lives within you—
No road noises, no people's part.
The world may come crashing down on you.

You will have the whole world to pursue—
No restraints, no control of start—
If you fall in love that is true.

No one has control, it is true.
If you do, then you are too smart.
The world may come crashing down on you.

Mend broken hearts; use tonic glue.
Remember that God lives in hearts,
If you fall in love that is true.
The world may come crashing down on you!

House of God

They say the heart is the abode of God,
Yet the heart remains breakable.
You should not break the house of God.

It's soft and not to ramrod;
Pliable, yet it is brittle
They say the heart is the abode of God

Break everything above the sod,
But leave the heart to be revealed.
You should not break the house of God.

He is above manly façade,
Not curbed by the walls of a bethel.
They say the heart is the abode of God.

He is deserving of applause.
Hold him pure and impeccable.
You should not break the house of God.

Nothing happens without his nod.
In God's house each thing is vital.
They say the heart is the abode of God.
You should not break the house of God.

PART 2

Mother Nature

Nature

Nature is always singing love.
Be with nature, and you will see
They go together hand and glove.

Soothing and attractive as a dove,
It is as clear as it can be:
Nature is always singing love.

In the cases listed above,
Look around you and you will see
They go together hand and glove.

In warm sun, sit under the olive
Or in floral vale, and you'll see
Nature is always singing love.

Nature makes you feel, all above,
Extremely happy and in glee,
They go together hand and glove.

Give it a chance; be in nature's love.
You will feel absolutely free.
Nature is always singing love.
They go together hand and glove.

Air

Birds and kites drift on its shoulder.
They may tumble, free without weight.
It may be seen when it makes flags flutter.

Birds glide and play without a stir
In open space, without a gate.
Birds and kites drift on its shoulder.

It keeps soul and body together.
In its absence we can't operate.
It may be seen when it makes flags flutter.

The nose can detect noxious odors;
It fades as we reach the pearly gates.
Birds and kites drift on its shoulder.

A hidden sustainer of ardor
Keeps guards from leading you to fate.
It may be seen when it makes flags flutter.

It is a gift of nature.
Keep it clean like a placid lake.
Birds and kites drift on its shoulder.
It may be seen when it makes flags flutter.

Bluebonnets

Vast stretches of highways abut
Accent of Indian paintbrush
Over color of bluebonnets.

A show of richly painted blankets,
Colors make painted carpet blush;
Vast stretches of highways abut.

Scattered the Divine Artist's palettes
For us to use, colors so lush
Over color of bluebonnets.

When they have the feel of velvet,
To see beauty you have to rush;
Vast stretches of highways abut.

For the tourist, it's a magnet.
You have to be there before the rush
Over color of bluebonnets.

It's all beauty; there is no smut.
Bring your palette and a paintbrush.
Vast stretches of highways abut
Over color of bluebonnets.

A Wall of Passion Fruit Vines

I watched it move to the top of the fence:
Passion fruit vine, a slow crawl
Hanging from wires along the fence.

It slithered like a reptile, no pretense,
Without any fight or a brawl.
I watched it move to the top of the fence.

In time, the arbor grew intense;
Painted blue flowers on a green shawl
Hanging from wires along the fence.

Tendrils twined around the expanse—
The fence's size had limited the sprawl.
I watched it move to the top of the fence.

The green vine grew extremely dense,
With fruit like a hanging Christmas ball,
Hanging from wires along the fence.

Enthralled to see this green and immense,
Almost perfect flamboyant wall,
I watched it move to the top of the fence,
Hanging from wires along the fence.

Wintry Blizzard

Nature does not always simper;
If angered, it shows an ugly face.
Sometimes it blows hard and brings a blizzard.

At times, cold wind makes us go *brrr*.
Though by far it keeps a happy face,
Nature does not always simper.

It blows, and you run for the cellar;
Then gentle myrrh hits you in the face.
Sometimes it blows hard and brings blizzard.

If it gets in a whirling stir,
Whirlwinds may lift your trees and place.
Nature does not always simper.

Embrace nature, and it will purr,
Let fauna flourish, and make space.
Wind can blow hard and make a blizzard.

Flower will bloom, and birds will whir.
It will be time for the spring's grace.
Nature does not always simper.
Sometimes it blows hard and brings a blizzard.

A Stray Wisp

A stray wisp from the vegetable garden
Reminds me of its native place of dawn.
Let us spread pixie dust in the basin.

Take me back to the place of libation
Where the wind sways bristles of the wheat awn,
A stray wisp from the vegetable garden.

In the breadbasket of the world, often
Instead of sunrays, missiles bring in dawn.
Let us spread pixie dust in the basin.

Flawed seed is sown by the man toting a gun.
Since Cain and Abel, man has killed thereon
A stray wisp from the vegetable garden.

It paints a flawed picture for human children
And does not put out the fire raging on.
Let us spread pixie dust in the basin.

Hold hands, and to fragrant wisp we hearken.
Spawn sweetness, and let bygones be bygones,
A stray wisp from the vegetable garden.
Let us spread pixie dust in the basin!

Nature Does Not Forget Polluters

There is no one to blame but sheer neglect.
Signs that harbinger the future are here.
Remember that Nature doesn't forget.

Let us our past recall and not reject.
Years of neglect will take time to clear.
We have no one to blame but sheer neglect.

The time to act is here; let's not make a wrong bet.
Let's not allow the heat of sun to sear.
Remember that Nature doesn't forget.

It's our abode; we cannot play roulette.
Still, there is time to stop what seems so near.
We have no one to blame but sheer neglect.

We have a duty to fix what we wrecked.
Nature's laws are dear, and we cannot veer.
Remember that Nature doesn't forget.

Years of neglect will take time to reverse,
But we cannot permit things to get worse.
We have no one to blame but sheer neglect.
Remember that Nature doesn't forget!

PART 3

Civilization

Humility

It was not very long ago:
On rainy days, you shared dry wood,
A gesture that bounced to and fro.

You did not hesitate to show
That you were thankful for the wood
And allowed your gratitude to grow.

For your kindness you would not crow;
The words were not misunderstood.
It was not meant just for show.

If sorrow fell upon you, though,
You could depend on the neighborhood.
It was not very long ago.

For emotional overflow,
Your pleas were heard and understood.
It was not meant just for show.

To show politeness, you did bow.
In your own matters, you were good.
It was not very long ago.
It was not meant just for show.

Not Long Ago

It was not very long ago
That people lived as people should.
It was not meant just for show.

If they needed to, they could borrow.
On cold days, neighbors gave chopped wood.
It was not very long ago.

Doors were open; no one said no.
Words were not misunderstood.
It was not meant just for show.

When told to play, their faces would glow.
Respect for the elders was understood.
It was not very long ago.

They used home remedies such as aloe.
Everyone knew what was good.
It was not meant just for show.

Kids frolicked in the white snow
Or sat by blazing firewood.
It was not very long ago.
It was not meant just for show.

Modern Cities

Molten ore molded into a globe
Competes with the organic space
And modifies the current nature of the orb.

Besmeared by the arrogant probe,
Proliferating fake spaces,
Molten ore is molded into a globe.

The ambition to modify the globe,
Birthing meaningless empty space,
Modifies the current state of the orb.

We should limit the extent of the probe
And think about a novel base:
Molten ore molded onto the globe.

Take a different look at the globe:
To initiate a newer race
Modifies the current state of the orb.

We have destroyed the current globe.
We should look for a different space.
Molten ore molded onto the globe
Modifies the current state of the orb.

Traffic on LBJ and Highway 75

In a labyrinth of highways crisscrossing
From every side at different levels,
No one knows where the others are going.

Riding the vehicles which are moving,
Size is measured in number of axles
In a labyrinth of highways crisscrossing.

Passing the other to prove he is king
Without fear of injury or libel,
No one knows where the other is going.

Hormones raging, car accelerating,
Changing lanes without looking at panels
In a labyrinth of highways crisscrossing—

Racing shouldn't be about gloating.
A poem should leave us with thoughts to mull.
No one knows where the others are going.

Highway driving is not meant for dragging.
Losing a friend is painful for us mortals.
In a labyrinth of highways crisscrossing,
No one knows where the others are going.

Smut on Earth

If we run out of land on earth,
There is enough space in orbit.
Let's hop to a close place of mirth.

We should explore a place for rebirth
And a cargo without bullets,
If we run out of land on Earth.

Man is exploring space near Earth.
Make certain we have no arms glut.
Let's hop to a close place of mirth.

There is no dearth of places of worth,
But first we should look at our own smut,
If we run out of land on Earth.

We can look for a new place of mirth,
If Earth is taken up with smut.
Let's hop to a close place of mirth.

Let's not rush to leave our place on Earth.
Unless we cleanse the earth of smut
If we run out of land on Earth,
Let's hop to a close place of mirth.

Wonderful Place

Our world could be a wonderful place,
Except for the mischief of man.
Let us give the world a peaceful space.

But for man's nefarious race,
If mankind could change (and it can),
Our world could be a wonderful place.

If we would cater to its base,
It would have a happier clan.
Let us give the world a peaceful space.

The entire rancor and the chase
Should have no place in the plan—
Our world could be a wonderful place,

If we control the human race
And follow a peaceable plan.
Let us give the world a peaceful space.

If humankind can live with grace
And learn to live like a free man,
Our world could be a wonderful place.
Let us give the world a peaceful space

PART 4

Wars

Baggage of a Leader

Flames of hate need to be put out.
A raging fire does not need stoked.
Informed heads should know the ins and outs.

If it rages, scorched earth will be a rout.
Stop it before it burns roadblocks.
Flames of hate need to be put out.

Mute the slogans that are too far out
Before they further provoke.
Informed heads should know the ins and outs.

Leave provocative placards out.
Minimize the use of hot "pokes."
Flames of hate need to be put out.

Until the plant is rooted well and stout,
Let us shed the reptilian cloak.
Sane heads should know the ins and outs.

Allow not the rancor to sprout.
Let humanity be unwrapped.
Flames of hate need to be put out.
Informed heads should know the ins and outs.

Human Fallacies

This was once a busy street in the town,
Now covered with lifeless, mangled bodies,
Devastating carnage in a small town.

It is the madness of single crazed clown,
Aimless desecration of man like fleas.
This was once a busy street in the town.

Buildings stand pockmarked and edifice browned.
Human corpses are covering alleys—
Devastating carnage in a small town.

The playful hamlet resembles a ghost town,
Proving that at times man can go crazy.
This was once a busy street in the town.

Human beings may need to further clamp down,
Unless we stop the pursuit of fallacies—
Devastating carnage in a small town.

Let's remember before the next clampdown.
Let us take care of our own fallacies.
This was once a busy street in the town;
Devastating carnage in a small town.

Bombing in Ukraine

With a high-pitched squeal and a streak in the sky,
A bomb scored a hit where children played.
Few left their homes, not knowing why.

War stalled because the world heard their cry.
Killings had the people dismayed
With a high-pitched squeal and a streak in the sky.

Some explained killings on the sly.
Most of the people appeared dazed.
Few left their homes, not knowing why.

Intense use of power from the sky
Caused the whole world to see people slayed
With a high-pitched squeal and a streak in the sky.

It would be mindless to stand by.
Hope and pray that we don't act crazed.
Few left their homes, not knowing why.

How many more will have to die?
When will be the leadership swayed
With a high-pitched squeal and a streak in the sky?
Few left their homes, not knowing why.

Day Six of War

An unprovoked war of insane mind
Sent tanks rumbling towards Ukraine
Under cloud of artillery's grind,

Attacked a country unaligned,
Inflicting on millions grave pain
In an unprovoked war of insane mind.

Its due place America will find,
But she will leave shackles behind
Under cloud of artillery's grind.

What we have lost, we shall find:
Unity, discipline, and brain
In an unprovoked war of insane mind.

No loss, but everything to gain:
But it will take control of rein
Under cloud of artillery's grind.

Let us think with the right mind,
Allow the nation to heal its blain
In an unprovoked war of insane mind
Under cloud of artillery's grind.

Day Eleven of War

Oil wellheads keep nodding all right
In snow-white oil fields of Russia,
Refusing a no-fly with might.

Weak Ukraine cannot face the might.
The world is lulled by Russian hula.
Oil wellheads keep nodding all right.

The world has tuned into Ukraine's plight,
Pleading to stop this mania
Refusing a no-fly with might.

A man plays piano through the night—
Save his children from losing Papa.
Oil wellheads keep nodding all right.

Pleas fall on deaf ears of might
Determined to hold to a dogma,
Refusing a no-fly with might.

"Never" is not before His might;
The transgressor will burn in lava.
Oil wellheads keep nodding all right,
Refusing a no-fly with might.

Doomsday Clock at 100 Seconds before Midnight

Unbearably painful to pen,
Mothers consoling the children,
Man is cruel to other men.

Father carrying mangled son,
Tired face, tears flowing, shows the ruin,
Unbearably painful to pen.

Tales of man's sadism towards men,
Baffled eyes watch metal dragons;
Man is cruel to other men.

From buildings where once lived some men
Smoke billows, and the world is stunned—
Unbearably painful to pen.

Wars bring out the worst in most men.
Man should have regard for children.
Man is cruel to other men.

Nuclear war may spare no one,
Leaving scorched earth and some ruins.
Unbearably painful to pen,
Man is cruel to other men.

What Wins a War?

Grit carries the day in a war
And resolve to fight for the cause.
It isn't the head count that wins a war.

War can't be won by a lone czar.
It is the passion for a cause.
Grit carries the day in a war.

The result does not hinge on one's stars
Or how you entertain in spas.
It isn't the head count that wins a war.

Ammo will go only so far.
The rest depends on the weight of the cause.
Grit carries the day in a war.

Do not worry about your scars.
The enemy will exploit your flaws.
It isn't the head count that wins a war.

Act thoughtfully; reach for the stars.
It has a lot to do with the cause.
Grit carries the day in a war.
It isn't the head count that wins a war

Resolve of Fighters

It is not the head count that wins a war
But the resolve of fighters for the cause.
Grit seems to carry the day in any war.

Wars cannot simply be won by a czar;
It is passion of fighters for a cause.
It is not the head count that wins a war.

You may think results depend on the stars
Or how you treat generals in the spas.
Grit seems to carry the day in any war.

Ammunition will go only so far;
The rest depends on the weight of the cause.
It is not the head count that wins a war.

Do worry about the ones who carry stars.
The enemy will exploit their flaws.
Grit seems to carry the day in any war.

Act thoughtfully and reach for the stars.
Remember, it has lot to do with the cause.
It is not the head count that wins a war.
Grit seems to carry the day in any war.

PART 5

Looking Back

Land of Punjab

In the productive rural land
Of Punjab, greenery abounds,
But there are flat bellies and tired hands.

Workers go home with empty hands.
Their bellies need a few extra pounds
In the productive rural land.

They weed the crops with their bare hands.
There are no more smiles to be found,
But there are flat bellies and tired hands

In a breadbasket with a past so grand,
Boasting of a past that was sound
In the productive rural land.

Fertile soil had been always manned;
Now labor is not to be found,
But there are flat bellies and tired hands.

Hands that tilled land now play in the band.
With hot sun the skin has been browned.
There are sunken bellies and tired hands
In the productive rural land.

Memories

In the fertile Punjab province,
Glistening tracks of mustard gold
Give the landscape a golden rinse.

Sunshine of summer helps grow quince.
Land appears to have sprouted gold
In the fertile Punjab province.

Five rivers fertilize the province.
Everything grows fast, like mold.
Give the landscape a golden rinse.

Rivers bring silt to the province;
Fertilizers you may withhold
In the fertile Punjab province.

Monsoon rains give the province a good rinse,
And the rains grow crops manifold,
Giving the landscape a golden rinse.

In the fertile Punjab province,
Sunshine paints color to behold.
In the fertile Punjab province,
Give the landscape a golden rinse.

Reminiscing

In those rare moments of my dream,
I saw my youth with fondness, and
I was barefoot in rain, it seems.

Dressed in loincloth of simple theme,
I ran till I was away from land,
In those rare moments of my dream.

I rowed in a small boat upstream,
And there was no one to lend a hand.
I was barefoot in rain, it seems.

I was carrying mango ice cream,
Homemade; I lugged it around in one hand
In those rare moments of my dream.

I rowed the boat against the stream,
Playing music over broadband.
I was barefoot in rain, it seems.

Moon drifting along the stream,
Crops waved from the distant farmland.
In those rare moments of my dream,
I was barefoot in rain, it seems.

Old House

Why did I come back all the way
To an old house I once occupied?
This is no more a place to stay.

No one has ever come to stay.
I sat in the entrance and sighed.
Why did I come back all the way?

To dodge Covid I came to stay.
I sat in the door and cried.
This is no more a place to stay.

I did not have to come this way
Just to stay quiet and to hide.
Why did I come back all the way?

I could have saved a busy day.
Instead I stayed and cried and cried.
This is no more a place to stay.

This was quite a wasted day!
I waited till the tears had dried.
Why did I come back all the way?
This is no more a place to stay

Where is My Idol?

On a glum day, I bowed my head in shame,
Recollected images of then and now.
Comparison did not fit in the frame.

I looked at the past; my eyes welled in shame.
The approaching storm was too thick to plow.
On a glum day, I bowed my head in shame.

Among ruins were pieces of truth and fame.
Concern for the needy was their daily chow.
Comparison did not fit in the frame.

Helping the needy to be paid was the aim,
The blind holding the hands of the one with eyes now.
On a glum day, I bowed my head in shame.

Teach trade instead of people living lame.
Teach them to learn a trade, and teach them how.
Comparison did not fit in the frame.

My eyes were blurred by the cloud of blame.
Wipe the cloud off faces, and give them know-how.
On a glum day, I bowed my head in shame.
Comparison did not fit in the frame.

PART 6

Life's Fragility

Extra Weight

His pants were now extremely tight,
If you could hear his morning rants.
Wearing pants by himself was a fight.

With more fat, his pants did not fit right.
He still wanted to wear the same pants;
His pants were now extremely tight.

Blubber did exert its own might,
Hung over the belt in any stance.
Wearing pants by himself was a fight.

He did not think it could be right;
He thought it was merely his stance—
His pants were now extremely tight.

He thought to hide: it was all right
If he sat to eat, but wearing pants
By himself was a real fight.

He tried to put up a good fight;
He sucked in to be a smarty-pants.
His pants were now extremely tight.
Wearing pants by himself was a fight.

Genetic Disorder

I wrote a villanelle on Sunday.
Weekends are busy for doctors.
I wrote the story on a busy day.

I heard the story on Friday,
And my mind had a stormy stir.
I wrote a villanelle on Sunday.

This story is not heard every day:
A family member had cancer.
I wrote the story on a busy day.

The genes can sometime go astray.
It was a genetic disorder.
I wrote a villanelle on Sunday.

In this stray act, one has no say.
Genes mutate and cause the cancer.
I wrote the story on a busy day.

Choosing your parents is the solution,
But on this you have no say.
I wrote a villanelle on Sunday.
I wrote the story on a busy day.

Man's Quiddities

There is no logic for man's quiddities.
If I wonder, it makes me lose my wits.
I hear simple accounts, which are flimsy.

Some are explained by genetic vagaries.
Nothing is glossy or exactly fits.
There is no logic for man's quiddities.

Some ideas are baffling and fuzzy,
You will be hard-pressed to find a good fit.
I hear simple accounts that are flimsy.

But the mere thought makes me dizzy.
If you note there is a plethora of twits,
There is no logic for man's quiddities.

Let brains tease out any inequities.
It may be suitable to sit on it.
I hear simple accounts that are flimsy.

In some you may find similarity.
It is hard to find a pattern that fits.
There is no logic for man's quiddities.
I hear simple accounts, which are flimsy.

The Challenge of Covid-19

There was no vaccine at the scene.
There was no medical cure around.
Suddenly a lot of Covid was seen.

Hospitals were bursting at the seams.
Coughing was a common sound.
There was no vaccine at the scene.

Many were placed in quarantine.
Wheezing sounds were all around.
Suddenly a lot of Covid was seen.

People drowned at the scene,
Not enough oxygen on hand.
There was no vaccine at the scene.

There were moans behind the screen.
Too few caregivers could be found.
Suddenly a lot of Covid was seen.

Too many to care for at the scene,
Not enough respirators around,
There was no vaccine at the scene—
Suddenly a lot of Covid was seen.

The Menace of Covid-19

You need not do it for my sake.
Remember, mankind feels the heat.
It's a grim virus, not a fake.

Give mankind a well-deserved break.
This rogue virus you can defeat.
You need not do it for my sake.

You may be convinced it is fake.
Go to a morgue; look under the sheet.
It's a grim virus, not a fake.

It is real, and not just a fake.
No one is safe, even the elite.
You need not do it for my sake.

Go to the ER, and you will quake.
This vile bug can be hard to beat.
It's a grim virus, not a fake.

Buckle up your shoes, for man's sake.
If you wait, it won't be a feat.
You need not do it for my sake.
It's grim virus, not a fake.

Life

Everyone has to go one day.
Limited extensions are allowed:
A change in eating habits may extend your stay.

But one question about that extra stay:
Is it worth skipping the good food?
Everyone has to go one day.

One's legacy, however, stays.
It's important how you are viewed.
A change in eating habits may extend your stay.

The entire meaningless, trendy fray
Has been the reason for life being skewed.
Everyone has to go one day.

Then why fear leaving today?
The world is getting so far skewed
A change in eating habits may extend the stay.

Let us face the facts, come what may:
What you do see is a prelude.
Everyone has to go one day.
A change in eating habits may extend your stay.

Life's Sanctity

It's a death knell for humanity
When corpses are defiled on land
With the loss of life's sanctity.

It began with one man's insanity
To annex additional land.
It's a death knell for humanity.

Averse to man's need to be free,
The false perception of a strong hand
With the loss of life's sanctity

Stabs to quell man's need to be free,
From a ruler to a farmhand.
It's a death knell for humanity.

Man will keep his right to be free;
He will always fight for the homeland
With the loss of life's sanctity,

No loss of the passion to be free,
May it be sand or fertile land.
It's a death knell for humanity
With the loss of life's sanctity.

Hope

The sky is always dark before dawn,
Just as hope follows despair.
Once the curtain lifts, it is dawn.

Life renews with springs of a fawn.
A lifetime is a circular affair.
The sky is always dark before dawn.

A cloudy day shouldn't make you frown.
The rain will end, and the day become fair.
Once the curtain lifts, it is dawn.

It's busy on life's autobahn;
There is no moment for a scare.
The sky is always dark before dawn.

Do not allow yourself to be put upon;
Do not lose your pizzazz or flair.
Once the curtain lifts, it is dawn.

Put spring in your gait like fawn;
Instead of turtle, be a hare.
The sky is always dark before dawn.
Once the curtain lifts, it is dawn.

Length of Life is Controlled by the Telomere

What is borrowed for a lifetime?
Length is engraved in the telomere;
It is on loan for a fixed time,

Lent to us by nature at inception.
Where may we end up? Life will steer
What is borrowed for a lifetime.

There are allowances for good times
And deterrents for a bad career.
It is on loan for a fixed time.

There is a limit to extensions.
Length may be varied—that is clear.
What is borrowed for a lifetime?

Nature gave it us at inception,
Gave us elements that were dear.
It is on loan for a fixed time.

The telomere controls lifespan;
It takes control and does not veer.
What is borrowed for a lifetime?
It is on loan for a fixed time.

A Task Well Done

*A villanelle written at the demise of the
mother of a good friend of mine*

Mourn not the passage of your mother:
Extol her for doing her part.
Light a candle and make the world brighter.

She bore pains with a nice laughter
That came from within a mother's heart.
Mourn not the passage of your mother.

Don't allow what she lit to flicker.
She knew you would carry the part.
Light a candle and make the world brighter.

There is a burden on your shoulders:
What she left for you is your part.
Mourn not the passage of your mother.

With her gone, this world has less myrrh.
Now is a good time to make a start.
Light a candle and make the world brighter.

Now it's time to take it further.
With grace she has performed her part.
Mourn not the passage of your mother.
Light a candle and make the world brighter.

Printed in the United States
by Baker & Taylor Publisher Services